Can We Protect People from Natural Disasters?

Catherine Chambers

raintree

a Capstone company — publishers for children

Raintree is an imprint of Capstone Global Library Limited, a company incorporated in England and Wales having its registered office at 7 Pilgrim Street, London, EC4V 6LB – Registered company number: 6695582

www.raintree.co.uk
myorders@raintree.co.uk

Edited by Helen Cox Cannons
Designed by Steve Mead
Original illustrations © Capstone Global Library Limited 2015
Illustrated by HL Studios, Witney, Oxon
Picture research by Tracy Cummins
Production by Helen McCreath
Originated by Capstone Global Library Limited
Printed and bound in China by CTPS

ISBN 978 1 406 29072 1
18 17 16 15 14
10 9 8 7 6 5 4 3 2 1

British Library Cataloguing in Publication Data
A full catalogue record for this book is available from the British Library.

Acknowledgements
We would like to thank the following for permission to reproduce photographs: We would like to thank the following for permission to reproduce photographs: Alamy: © Guy Croft SciTech, 15, © Kevin Foy, 19, © Roy Conchie, 16; Capstone Press: 26, HL Studios, 4, 20, 31; Corbis: © ANDREW BIRAJ/Reuters, 8; Getty Images: Alain BUU/Gamma-Rapho, 13, Chip HIRES/Gamma-Rapho, 30, Davie Hinshaw/Charlotte Observer/MCT, 38, GAMMA/Gamma-Rapho, 6, INDRANIL MUKHERJEE/AFP, 34, Joe Raedle, 28, Mario Tama, 25, 29, Matt Cardy, 32, Matt Stroshane, 39, RAVEENDRAN/AFP, 18, SEYLLOU DIALLO/AFP, 35, TED ALJIBE/AFP, 21, YOSHIKAZU TSUNO/AFP, 17; NOAA: 22; Shutterstock: Ashley Whitworth, 37, J. Helgason, 12, Jag_cz, Cover, Janelle Lugge, 5, Jeffrey T. Kreulen, 11, jessicakirsh, 9, leonello calvetti, Cover, lexaarts, 41, Minerva Studio, 27, Prometheus72, 14, Repina Valeriya, 36, Richard Whitcombe, 10, Silken Photography, 33; Wikimedia: Jocelyn Augustino/FEMA, 23.

We would like to thank Professor Daniel Block for his invaluable help in the preparation of this book.

Every effort has been made to contact copyright holders of material reproduced in this book. Any omissions will be rectified in subsequent printings if notice is given to the publisher.

Contents

Some words are shown in bold, **like this**. You can find out what they mean by looking in the glossary.

What are natural disasters?

Fearsome floods, desperate droughts, violent volcanoes and shuddering earthquakes are all natural disasters. We hear about them happening all over the world. We learn how they cause death, devastation and disruption. But what is a natural disaster?

A natural disaster is an extreme weather or geological event. It overwhelms the defences that people have built to stop it. Normal natural weather forces such as wind, rain, sun and snow at their extremes become hurricanes, floods, droughts and blizzards. Mild earth tremors and gently oozing lava in remote places are harmless geological events. However, large earthquakes and explosive volcanoes pose a threat to the people living in the way of them.

⟩ Many parts of the world are at great risk from natural disasters. Risks are considered to be human deaths, destruction and economic harm.

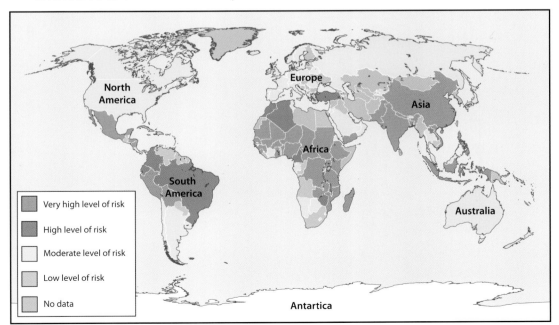

- Very high level of risk
- High level of risk
- Moderate level of risk
- Low level of risk
- No data

North America

Europe

Asia

Africa

South America

Australia

Antartica

The European Commission declares a natural disaster when an event causes 10 or more deaths and affects the lives of at least 100 people. The World Health Organization describes it as a "serious disruption of the functioning of a community ... causing widespread human, material, economic or environmental losses." A national government will declare a **state of emergency** or call for international assistance.

> " We have altered so many natural systems so dramatically, their ability to protect us from disturbances is greatly diminished. "
>
> Janet N. Abramovitz, Senior Researcher, Worldwatch Institute, Washington DC, USA

After a natural disaster, many questions are asked. Could people have been better warned and rescue teams more prepared? Could people have been better protected? How long has it taken to recover? Was it caused by human decisions?

≫ Could this forest fire caused by lightning, in drought-stricken Australia, have been prevented? Does human activity make droughts worse?

Did you know?

In 2012, the International Monetary Fund (IMF) found that between 2010 and 2011, 700 natural disasters were registered worldwide. They affected more than 450 million people.

Did you know?

Sometimes we create human-made disasters on top of natural ones. When a massive **tsunami** hit Japan in 2011, a **nuclear fuel** power plant was badly damaged. People have not returned to the surrounding area because the leaked nuclear fuel let out massive amounts of harmful **radiation**.

What are the effects of natural disasters?

Shattered lives, battered buildings and flattened habitats are some of the immediate effects of natural disasters. **Infrastructures** are also destroyed, including hospitals, roads, railways, airports and **telecommunications**. This destruction delays rescue and recovery. People who need medical care are forced to wait, so their health worsens. Food runs out, people are weakened and so are more likely to become ill. Broken water supplies and sewage systems bring disease.

The longer-term effects include displacement. This is when people are forced to leave their homes, schools and work. In farming communities, crops and grazing land are ruined, which badly damages local economies. In the later stages of a natural disaster, some people are too frightened or too poor to return and rebuild their area.

How do we measure natural disasters?

Measuring natural disasters gives us information that will help protect people from further natural disasters in the future. It shows us how to help people at each stage after the disaster, too. How is this done? Firstly, scientists measure the physical nature of the disaster. For example, how wide was the hurricane? How strong were the winds? How high were the ocean waves that hit the shore? How long did the disaster last? The second set of measurements shows the impact of the natural disaster on people, buildings, infrastructures and the economy. It also shows how much money it costs to make things better.

Scientists continue to measure a natural disaster for many years after it happened. They use new developments in mathematics, mapping and **computer models** to bring information up to date. So we now know that some natural disasters that happened in the past are even worse than we first thought.

Is it easy to protect people from natural disasters?

It can be hard to protect people from natural disasters where it is difficult to predict their strength, duration and exact location. However, as you can see from the map on page 4, there are parts of the world where natural disasters often occur. Therefore, scientists can concentrate on predicting disasters for these areas.

Predicting disasters helps us to prepare for them. Engineers can design strong buildings and barriers. Or they can deliver sources of water where drought often occurs. Emergency experts can set up warning systems. They can prepare rescue teams, equipment, and plans of action and recovery.

HERO OR VILLAIN?

How natural are natural disasters? Are we making weather disasters worse by contributing to climate change? Are we causing more earth tremors through mining and drilling? Should we stop living in the path of natural disasters? Do all these human activities make it harder to predict natural disasters and protect people from them?

⩔ Bangladesh's yearly floods are needed so that crops can be planted. But it is hard to protect people from drowning in large floods, and from the diseases that can be carried in water.

What makes protection harder?

Some disasters happen in developing countries, which cannot afford to protect themselves or carry out effective rescue and recovery. Others occur where war has already disrupted lives and destroyed infrastructures. Governments and international media sometimes do not report natural disasters in these areas early enough. This makes disasters very difficult to handle. As we can see below, though, richer nations are sometimes no better prepared than poorer ones.

Eyewitness

"We broke our way out through the rubble after the tornado hit. It's like we rose up into a war zone. Everything's gone here in Moore – even the two schools are flattened ... There was paper on the ground; schoolwork, and kids' stuff," said Toni Partin. "We walked just a little bit further ... and it got worse, and then the next street – completely gone. I've never seen anything like it. Five cars piled on top of each other."

Toni Partin, tornado survivor from Moore, Oklahoma, USA

Can we protect people from volcanoes?

How can we protect people from sudden volcanic eruptions that throw up clouds of ash and gas, rivers of hot mud, and **pyroclastic flows** that spit red-hot rocks, lava and burning air at 300 kilometres (184 miles) per hour? They can kill in seconds, and smother buildings, crops, services and infrastructures. What happens when slower volcanoes force people to move away? Can we help them rebuild their lives somewhere else?

⌄ This Indonesian village is constantly threatened by the steaming volcano behind it.

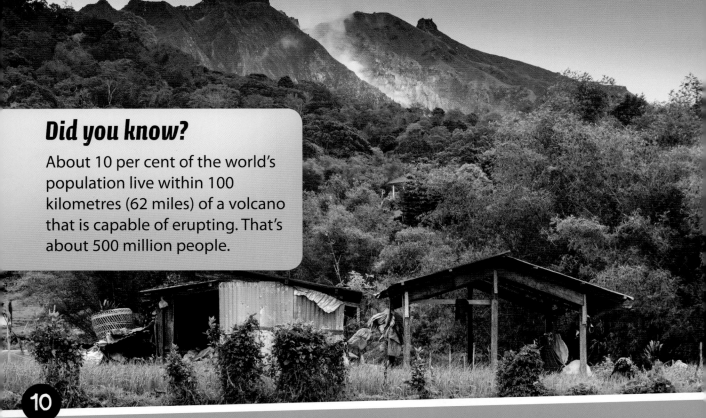

Did you know?

About 10 per cent of the world's population live within 100 kilometres (62 miles) of a volcano that is capable of erupting. That's about 500 million people.

⌃ An eruption of Mount Rainier could stop the city of Seattle, USA, in its tracks.

Why live near a volcano?

It is hard to protect large numbers of people living near or on a volcano. Why have they settled in such a dangerous place? The main reason is that volcanic slopes are well-drained and rich with **nitrogen** chemicals from broken-down volcanic matter. Nitrogen fertilizes the soil, helping crops to grow. Hardened volcanic lava makes good building material, too. So areas around volcanoes can be densely populated.

Huge cities, such as Seattle, have arisen at the feet of many dangerous volcanoes. This thriving, bustling US city lies only 87 kilometres (54 miles) from Mount Rainier. While it is currently **dormant**, this will not last forever. If it erupts and its 26 glaciers melt, then **lahars**, or boiling mudflows, will smother the surrounding lowland. **Hazard mapping** suggests that Seattle will be showered with hot ash. All those living in the volcano's shadow rely on science to pick up signals of volcanic activity. They rely on hazard mapping created by computers, which shows where lava is likely to flow. They depend on automatic warning sirens and planned evacuation pathways to help them escape. Will these measures work? Only time will tell!

Using science to help us

How can people be protected from volcanic eruptions? The answer lies in prediction and preparation. Volcanologists measure the tilt of the volcano's slopes to see if there is movement, and use seismometers to pick up tiny earth tremors. These are often the first signs of an eruption. Volcanologists also measure vibrations given off when rocks crack inside the volcano. This can indicate that magma is on the move towards the surface. Sensors inside and above the volcano measure any increase in **sulphur dioxide** gas and water vapour levels. High above Earth, space satellites use sensors to pick up tiny volcanic movements and infrared waves to detect rising heat levels from a restless volcano.

In addition, layers of volcanic rock from previous eruptions are analysed to see which way lava and lahars, or mudflows, are likely to run. This helps scientists create hazard maps and evacuation plans.

⌄ Billowing clouds of gas and ash rise into the air after an eruption. The ash can rise so high that it chokes aircraft engines.

Ash fall is very hard to clean up. It also pollutes rivers and destroys crops.

Eyewitness

In 1995, on the Caribbean island of Montserrat, residents awoke to a sickly smell, like rotten eggs. Then sulphur and ash exploded from the Soufriere Hills volcano and two-thirds of the islanders left. Shirley Spycalla stayed and still puts up with eruptions. "We've learned to live with it," she said. "What we've learned to do is to buy brooms, lots of brooms because when it starts to ash we clean it up right away."

How successful is the science?

A good example is when Mount Pinatubo in the Philippines erupted on 15 June 1991. It was the second-worst eruption of the 20th century. Hundreds of people died. But it could have been catastrophic. The Philippine Institute of Volcanology and Seismology (PHIVOLCS) and the US Geological Survey (USGS) had monitored Mount Pinatubo closely. Thousands of people were evacuated and property worth five times the amount spent on the science was saved.

Can we protect people from earthquakes?

We cannot yet predict earthquakes. We don't know how strong they will be or how long they will last. So how can we warn people and protect them?

There are thousands of earthquakes every year in earthquake zones around the world. The country of Japan alone experiences 1,500 each year and its capital city, Tokyo, is stirred by tremors every day! Some earthquakes are very small and last a few seconds. Others are massive and last several minutes. Aftershocks can hit for weeks, months or even years.

⌄ Earthquakes like this one, which hit Turkey in 1999, can be measured on different scales. The Richter Scale uses seismology to measure the speed of the amount of energy an earthquake releases.

BIOGRAPHY

**Professor Keiiti Aki
(1930–2005)**
Professor Keiiti Aki was a
geophysicist who developed
a way of measuring the
amount of energy released
by an earthquake. He
also analysed seismic
recordings carefully, to
find out more about the
origins and behaviour of
earthquakes. Keiiti Aki
founded the Southern
California Earthquake
Center, which continues
his work.

⌃ Professor Aki analysed seismographs,
like this one, which show the energy
of tremors.

Measuring earthquakes

Seismologists measure the strength of earthquakes as they happen. Then
they assess the damage caused by the earthquake. The data is put together
with our knowledge of faultlines, deep cracks in Earth's crust, where
earthquakes begin. From this, we can locate earthquake hotspots and draw
up hazard maps. This means we know roughly where people most need
evacuation plans and protective measures.

Scientists are improving earthquake detection all the time. At the moment,
instruments can give people up to 60 seconds to prepare, which is a
potentially life-saving amount of time. Scientists use seismometers to
measure movements that happen both deep underground or on Earth's
surface. These movements are converted into electrical signals which are
then sent to computers. These computers activate early warning systems
which help to save lives.

What happens after a warning signal?

The first pulse from an earthquake's source triggers earthquake warning systems. People grab their emergency packs and find a place of safety. The warning has given them a chance of protection from the slower but more damaging tremors that then shake and pull at Earth's surface. Automatic shutdown devices on lifts, escalators and other dangerous transporters kick in. Emergency services get ready for rescue and recovery.

Until help arrives, people try to survive on their emergency packs. These usually contain water, food, a first-aid kit, a radio that can run on batteries or a winding-handle, a torch, thermal blanket and a charged mobile phone.

Did you know?

Istanbul's Sabiha Gökçen International Airport terminal opened on 31 October 2009 and is now one of the world's largest earthquake-proof buildings. It was built to withstand a collossal earthquake measuring 8 on the Richter scale and to carry on working afterwards.

When an earthquake happens, it hits buildings, roads and bridges with massive underground sidekicks (tremors). Do people have any chance of survival in buildings not designed to withstand this? Many countries

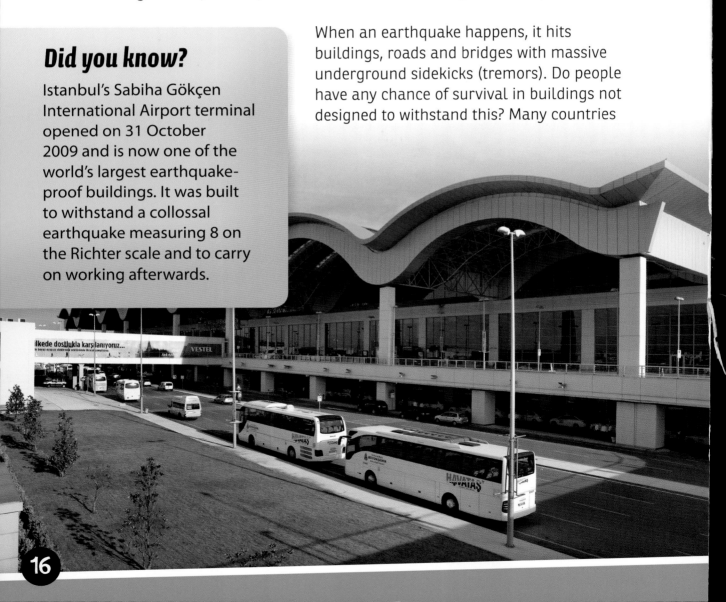

⏫ Children in Japan take part in regular earthquake drills, as you can see in the picture. The children know exactly what to do.

do not have enough money to construct earthquake-resistant buildings. However, where this is possible, even high-rise buildings should stay upright, depending on the size of the earthquake. They are built so that they can sway on their base, which stays firm. Buildings that are cemented to their base are too rigid and so crack up when waves of energy ripple through them.

So we can see that lives can be protected. But when will we get more warning of earthquakes happening? New studies of earthquake patterns will hopefully help. The Global Telemetred Seismograph Network is using satellite technology and computer links to create a worldwide earthquake study system deep beneath Earth's surface. This new project has not yet saved lives, but it is hoped that one day it will.

HERO OR VILLAIN?

Some warning systems are so sensitive to tremors that people are becoming tired of evacuation procedures. This negative reaction to warning systems is dangerous, as people will not respond quickly enough in an earthquake.

⌃ About a quarter of a million people were killed by the 2004 Boxing Day tsunami in countries along the Indian Ocean, from Malaysia in the east to Africa in the west.

Can people be protected from tsunami disasters?

A tsunami is a series of ocean waves that hurtle towards the shore. Most are caused by earthquakes either on land or deep under the sea. Their movement pushes against the water, creating enormous waves. A few tsunamis are set off by landslips that slide into the water, or a lava flow from a volcano. Once started, they travel extremely fast.

Eyewitness

Daniel Thebault witnessed the Boxing Day tsunami disaster in 2004: "We heard a roaring noise and could see ripples of frothy water bubbling up fast from the beach ... the bay emptied of water ... but then the sea started charging ahead again. Great big swathes of the beach are completely washed away ... and the coconut palms are five or six feet under water."

In the open ocean, tsunami waves can be hundreds of kilometres long but are usually only a metre high – that is, until they reach the shore. Then, in the shallow water they are thrust upwards and crash inland, causing death and devastation.

So how can people be protected? Satellite instruments can measure and track the height of the waves. In the United States, instruments that can detect changes in water pressure are being set along the seabed. The results are signalled to sensors on **buoys** floating on the water. From here, they are picked up by satellites and transmitted to warning centres. Automatic alarms or text-messaging systems tell people to move quickly to higher ground.

In the Pacific Ocean, where many tsunamis occur, there is the Tsunami Warning System (TWS), which is a network of earthquake and tsunami monitoring stations. However, this did not prevent the 2011 tsunami disaster in Japan, when a massive 9-magnitude earthquake triggered this monster tsunami.

⌄ Barriers are built along vulnerable coastlines to break up tsunami waves as they hit.

Can we protect people from hurricanes?

It is hard to protect people from the racing winds, torrential rain and thunderstorms of a hurricane. But what is a hurricane, and where does it come from?

What is a hurricane?

A hurricane is a tropical cyclone. This is a low, rotating system of clouds and thunderstorms that builds up speed and pressure over hundreds of kilometres. It develops over warm oceans in the hot tropical and subtropical regions of the world. Here, the warmth of the water creates moisture in the air that fuels the strength of the winds and the duration of the hurricane.

Diagram of the formation of a hurricane

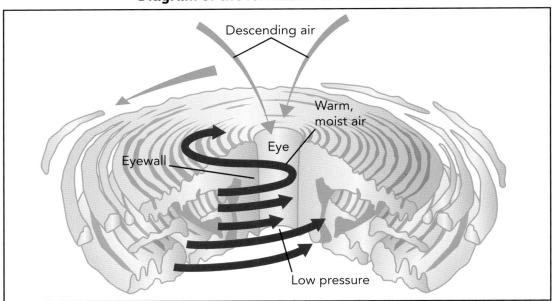

⌃ This diagram shows how the hurricane's warm, moist air rises continually around the calm eye of the storm, which has very low pressure. The winds whirl clockwise in storms south of the equator, and anti-clockwise north of the equator.

⋀ Typhoon Haiyan hit the Philippines in
November 2013 with the highest winds
ever recorded.

Hurricanes can strike with wind speeds of up to 249 kilometres (155 miles)
per hour. They batter islands and coastlines in the Caribbean, eastern and
southern coasts of the United States, and the northwest Pacific. Typhoons
are the same type of storm but hit vast lengths of eastern Asia's coastline.
In the Indian Ocean and South Pacific, these storms are called cyclones.

How can we predict a hurricane?

In the Atlantic, hurricanes happen every year from mid-May to the end
of November. We can see hurricanes building up as satellite instruments
can track their path and detect heat building up inside them. Aircraft can
fly into the storm system with instruments that measure the hurricane's
pressure, wind direction, temperature and humidity. We use a measure
called the Saffir–Simpson Scale to assess the damage they might cause.
Yet we still cannot protect people from major hurricanes, especially from
the storm surges that they bring.

⌃ Hurricane Katrina approached the southern coast of the United States and hit land on 29 August 2005.

What is a storm surge?

A storm surge is a huge, bulging ocean wave that can turn a hurricane into a natural disaster when it hits the shoreline. It is pushed up by winds that rage around the cyclone, and is helped a little by the extreme low pressure within the hurricane itself.

The wave can be as tall as a house, but its size depends on the shape and slope of the shoreline. The storm surge's height and speed, and the sheer weight of water can cause huge loss of life and damage to buildings and infrastructures.

A massive storm surge erodes beaches, destroys marinas, harbours and coastal roads, and topples buildings or damages their foundations. It floods estuaries and marshes with deadly concentrations of saltwater that kill wildlife and vegetation. Water, through its initial force and then its flooding, is the biggest cause of human death from a hurricane, even though the winds are very destructive, too. In 2005, 1,800 people were killed by Hurricane Katrina when it hit the US states of Louisiana, Mississippi and Alabama.

HERO OR VILLAIN?

Some forms of nature benefit from the storm surge! Coral creatures create long reefs that protect coastlines from heavy waves. Coral creatures lay their eggs and, when a storm surge hits, the eggs are spread out far and wide to create new areas of protective reef.

∨ The many deaths caused by Hurricane Katrina were because of the storm surge that, in some places, rose to over 8 metres (28 feet) above normal high tide levels.

How can technology help people prepare?

In hurricane and typhoon zones, scientists closely follow satellite tracking and weather updates. If a serious hurricane is brewing, automatic warning systems kick in. Alerts are now available on social networking sites, as well as radio and television. The American Red Cross has developed an app that tracks the hurricane and provides a one-touch "I'm safe" messaging system to family and friends. Within the app a toolkit provides a torch, strobe light and loud alarm to use in case you are buried under a building.

Technology may help people prepare, but how can they be protected from harm? Homes can be strengthened and built on stilts to withstand winds and floods. Storm shutters stop windows and doors from blowing in. Specially designed straps tie down roofs to prevent them from flying away. From the United States and Australia to Jamaica and Japan, strict building codes are in place so that new structures can withstand hurricane-force winds.

What about storm surges?

Let us return to New Orleans, where the storm surge from Hurricane Katrina easily washed over barriers called levees. New levees, floodwalls and pumps are now in place. However, New Orleans was built on natural lowland marshes that absorbed floodwaters. Would more marshland along the city's coastline protect people better?

> "Dunes, barrier islands, mangrove forests and coastal wetlands are natural 'shock absorbers' that protect against coastal storms. Forests, floodplains and wetlands, are 'sponges' that absorb floodwaters. Nature provides these services for free, and we should take advantage of them rather than undermining (destroying) them."
>
> Janet Abramovitz, Senior Researcher, Worldwatch

Herbert Seymour Saffir (1917–2007)
Herbert Saffir was a **structural engineer** who, with Robert Simpson, developed the first scale to measure hurricanes. It was based on wind speeds, the central pressure inside the hurricane and their effects on built structures and natural vegetation. The scale had five categories, from weak to devastating.

When New Orleans upgraded flood defences, they used computer modelling to simulate monster hurricanes. This picture shows the new floodwall running alongside the canal that was repaired after Hurricane Katrina.

Can we hide from tornadoes?

Tornadoes, or twisters, are funnels of whirling air that touch the ground at up to 113 kilometres (70 miles) per hour and suck up everything in their path. They pelt the earth with rain and hailstones while lightning flashes above. Can anyone escape the damage?

Thousands of tornadoes strike all over the world every year. But they cause the most destruction along Tornado Alley in the United States and in Bangladesh and eastern India. Tornadoes form from thunderstorms, especially in areas where dry and warm air meet and where moist air and cool air meet. Tornadoes can also form from hurricanes. Thirty-three tornadoes ran alongside Hurricane Katrina alone!

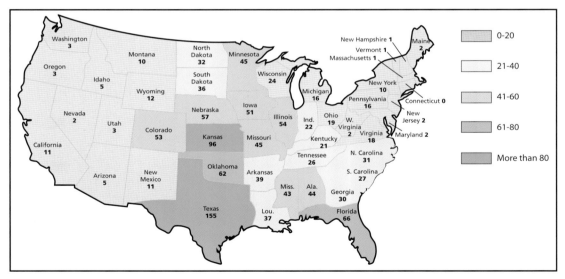

⌃ This diagram of the United States shows the number of tornadoes by state per year, between 1991 and 2010. The darker the states are coloured, the more tornadoes they have per year, Texas having easily the most at 155.

We do not exactly know what makes these whirling, sucking winds. At the moment, we can only measure their speed, width, duration and the amount of damage they do. All these combine to give us a reading on the Enhanced Fujita Scale (EF-Scale), which has five strengths. The fifth is the most powerful and describes tornadoes that can lift up houses, twist reinforced concrete bridges and throw cars up in the air to a distance of 100 metres (328 feet).

Detection

Can these tornadoes be detected so that people can be warned? In the United States, **Doppler Radar** equipment can detect likely tornado formation inside a thunderstorm. The radar tells when the winds begin to twist by the way they blow patterns of raindrops that show up on the radar screen. This information is fed into a computer simulation program that helps predict the tornado. At the same time, storm spotters identify dark, hanging bowl-shaped thunderclouds. They report it to the National Weather Service.

⌄ Storm chasers put their lives in danger to take pictures of tornadoes as the funnel hits the ground and begins to run.

BIOGRAPHY

Dr T. Theodore Fujita (1920–1998)
Dr T. Theodore Fujita was a **meteorologist** specializing in tornadoes, hurricanes, typhoons and thunderstorms. He helped develop the Fujita–Pearson Scale for classifying tornadoes.

Can people get out of the way?

When there's a tornado threat in the United States, the National Weather Service sends out an alert to the local emergency service in the tornado danger zone. Warning sirens are set off and messages are broadcast on radio and television. In many areas now, the information is picked up by smartphones from local mobile phone tower signals. A special ringtone identifies the hazard as a tornado and an automatic message gives advice.

How does this help? If people are warned in good time they can keep safe in a cellar, under a strong staircase or in a tornado shelter. These are reinforced concrete safe rooms built inside the home or in the garden.

⌃ Many homes in Tornado Alley are built from wood, so a strong tornado shelter is a potential life saver.

⌃ Much of Joplin, Missouri, USA, was flattened in the tornado of 23 May 2011, leaving 162 people dead and thousands injured. The damage to buildings and infrastructures cost $2.8 billion.

However, this is what happens in a perfect world. In reality, the price of building a storm shelter costs at least US$3,000. Local governments sometimes help with costs, but not always. What about the warning system? One of the worst recent disasters happened in Moore, Oklahoma. Here, the siren is not automatically activated. It still relies on someone pulling a handle!

In poor countries, governments struggle to invest in preventing a tornado disaster. They simply cannot afford it. So, people could be better protected from tornado disasters if more money was poured into warning systems and safer buildings.

> **Cars were crumpled up like tin cans. Businesses were levelled ... there are still people trapped inside. We've had tornadoes but this is one one the worst ever here.**
>
> Sara Ferguson, resident of Joplin

Can we protect people from flood disasters?

Floods can creep up slowly after long periods of steady rainfall. Or they can burst as flash floods from rivers swollen suddenly by torrential storms. They can be brought by tsunamis, storm surges or unusually high tides. Some floods last for a few days. Others can stay for months. But what turns a flood event into a flood disaster? Can people be protected from them?

We hear a lot of news about flooding in countries that do not expect it. But some parts of the world are flooded every year. One of these is Bangladesh. Bangladesh is regularly flooded from snow melting high in the Himalaya mountain range to the north. It is also flooded by heavy **monsoon** rains, and when high sea tides and high river levels occur at the same time.

⌄⌄ Most farmers in Bangladesh live in raised villages on the floodplains, which are called char lands.

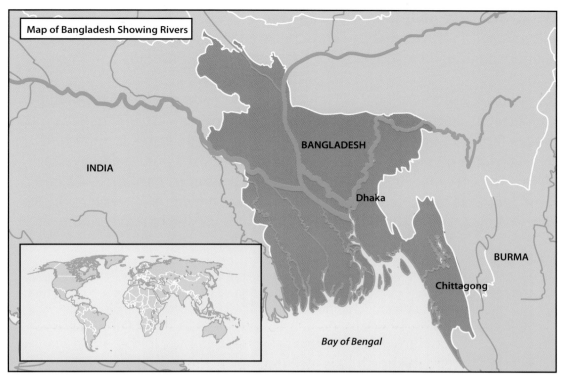

Map of Bangladesh Showing Rivers

INDIA

BANGLADESH

Dhaka

BURMA

Chittagong

Bay of Bengal

⌃ Most of Bangladesh is low-lying. The country sits where three major rivers meet.

Most people here live on the floodplains so that they can farm. Low levels of flooding are welcomed, as they **irrigate** fields that can then be planted with crops. The crops grow better after a flood. But many people die when floods are heavy and thousands lose their homes. In 2012, floodwater and landslides affected more than 5 million people in the floodplains. Crops were ruined and 360,000 homes damaged.

Did you know?

In Bangladesh, rice is the main food crop. Rice plants grow in water but are normally ruined if floodwater covers them completely. Scientists at the International Rice Research Institute in the Philippines have developed a variety of rice that can cope under water for at least 12 days.

What will help people in flood zones?

In Bangladesh, levees protect some char villages from flooding. Flood shelters built high on stilts provide some emergency housing.

What about flood warnings? We have seen that modern satellite technology connected to warning systems and text-messaging services are able to protect people faced with sudden disaster. However, in Bangladesh it is important to give people a long time to prepare themselves, their homes and livestock. Here, computer models now give early predictions of tropical cyclones and high tides that cause flooding. Hazard maps are drawn up for each of the 38 river management stations to see where local floodwaters might run.

In 2013, the UK's Meteorological Office predicted a dry winter. By February 2014, the heaviest rainfall ever recorded had flooded vast areas. Many people blamed the flooding on rivers and channels that had not been dredged for years.

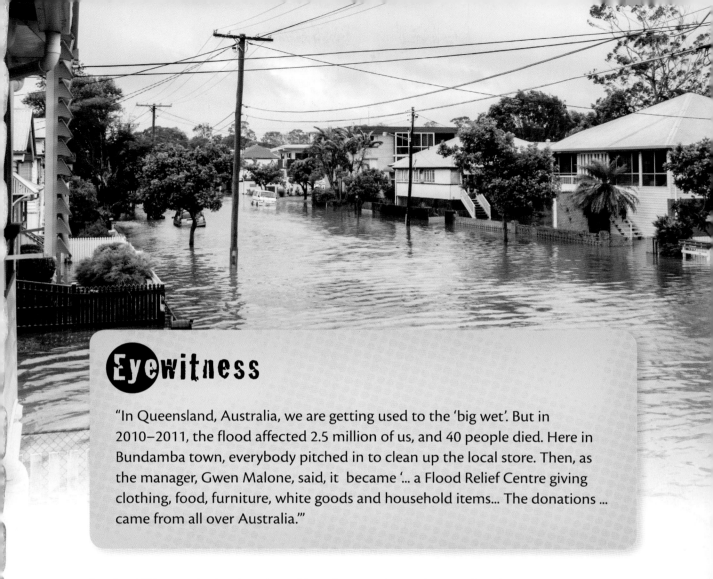

Eyewitness

"In Queensland, Australia, we are getting used to the 'big wet'. But in 2010–2011, the flood affected 2.5 million of us, and 40 people died. Here in Bundamba town, everybody pitched in to clean up the local store. Then, as the manager, Gwen Malone, said, it became '... a Flood Relief Centre giving clothing, food, furniture, white goods and household items... The donations ... came from all over Australia.'"

In the UK, people in the city of Leeds are also using technology and a very local approach to solve possible flooding. A small robotic boat is floated on the river that runs through the city. It carries **sonar equipment**, which records the shape of the underwater river bed. This shows where the river needs to be **dredged** and where higher flood defence walls should be built.

What about building with floods in mind? In the Netherlands, most people live below sea level Here, water is held back and controlled by a system of levees, drainage channels and canals. They have also designed buildings set on floating foundations that can rise with the floodwaters if flood defences fail.

Can we prevent drought disaster?

Drought is a long period of very dry conditions that occurs in a place that normally receives a regular amount of rainfall. It can last for months or even years. Streams, rivers and lakes dry up above ground and below. Natural vegetation shrivels up, and wild animals, crops and livestock die. In many poor parts of the world where drought hits, people also die. In all drought areas, the economy dips and development is held back.

Why do droughts happen?

Most droughts begin with weather systems that bring prolonged periods of high air pressure. High pressure gives bright blue skies and sunny days, but no clouds or rain.

⌄ In California, USA, cloud-seeding machines attached to aircraft scatter particles of silver iodide chemical into clouds to help rain form within them.

But what causes long periods of high pressure? Meteorologists have several theories. These include changes in ocean temperatures and the position of wide ribbons of air called jet streams, high up in the atmosphere. Many scientists point to climate change caused by burning fossil fuels.

Making drought worse

All around the world people have cleared natural vegetation such as forest and grassland to grow crops or take wood for building and fuel. They have drained wetlands and built over many of them. Natural vegetation and wetlands keeps moisture in the soil. They also release water vapour that rises and forms rainclouds. So replanting trees and restoring wetlands are two ways of helping to protect against drought.

⌄ The Sahel stretches south of the Sahara across Africa from west to east. Africa's Great Green Wall project aims to plant trees in this zone to help stop drought and increase moisture.

Did you know?

Between the 1930s and 1950s, large areas of the United States experienced long periods of drought. Between the 1980s and 1990s, there was unusual rainfall with short periods of drought. In the first 10 years of the 2000s, there was severe drought – and rainfall! How can we prepare when conditions change so often?

Protecting people from the hazards that drought can bring

Drought also brings increased numbers of pests such as locusts and crickets. These creatures eat crops weakened by lack of rain. Burrowing insects worm their way into crops, too.

66 (Sorghum) can grow on **marginal** land. A lot of our own crops can't. A year ago I was in Mozambique, and the corn looked terrible, but the sorghum was strong and tall. It doesn't need all these things that other plants need. 99

Dr Joachim Messing, Professor of Molecular Biology, USA

Chemical pesticides will kill some of these pests, but the chemicals can harm the environment and the atmosphere. Poorer farmers cannot afford them, either. So scientists have developed new crops that can grow well without needing much moisture, or that can resist pests.

What about changing the crop itself? We are used to eating corn and wheat cereals, which often fail in drought. So some farmers in Africa are turning back to traditional cereals such as sorghum and millet. These can grow in very dry areas without **artificial irrigation**, which often uses up very limited water sources.

Another effect of drought is the danger of forest fires, which can quickly spread across very dry scrubland and forest. Some are started by people but research in Canada has found that there, 45 per cent are started by lightning.

How can people be protected from forest fires? Fire can be slowed down by wide forest roadways, called breaks. These have no vegetation to fuel the flames. Also, satellite imaging can help firefighters to see how and where the fire is spreading.

HERO OR VILLAIN?

Forest fires can help some plants. They roast the seeds of tree species such as Australia's Bluegum eucalyptus. The heat helps the seeds to germinate and grow into new trees.

Can we prevent a deep-freeze disaster?

A sudden deep freeze brings blizzards, ice storms, snow drifts, thick ice and sub-zero temperatures. It can last for days or even weeks. How can people be protected from a deep-freeze disaster?

People in many countries expect a deep freeze in winter. They know how to prepare for it by stocking up with food, and fuel to keep their homes warm. They wrap up water pipes to stop water from freezing inside. They attach chains to car tyres so that they can grip frozen, slippery roads. Governments make sure that there is enough salt grit to melt snow and ice on roads. Snow ploughs are at the ready to clear deep snow drifts.

> **This is one of Mother Nature's worst kind of storms that can be inflicted on the South. That is ice. It is our biggest enemy.**
>
> Governor Nathan Deal of Georgia State, USA, February 2014

⌃ Some of Florida State's orange crop was affected by ice in 2014.

However, some people rarely experience extreme cold where they live and are unprepared if it hits. An unexpected deep freeze hit parts of Canada and the United States in the winter of 2013–2014. Perilous ice and snow conditions hit the southern states, where deep freezes are very rare, causing deaths and severe disruption to power supplies and road, rail and air services.

Many people in a deep-freeze disaster die in accidents such as snow **avalanches** on mountains, or road crashes from icy conditions. But some people, especially the elderly, die of hypothermia, or extreme cold.

So what can be done to protect people? Early warning is important. However, in the severe winter of 2013–2014, US meteorologists found it difficult to predict snow and ice storms accurately. Does this mean that we cannot protect people from all types of natural disasters?

Can we really protect people from natural disasters?

Some natural disasters are so sudden that it is hard to protect people from them. But protection from most disasters can be improved with better monitoring, prediction and warning systems. This means that people will be able to escape from them.

Protective architecture and engineering can improve people's chances of survival if they cannot get away. Victims of a disaster can recover faster if they are provided with food, shelter and good health care. They are able to rebuild their lives if homes and communication networks are quickly repaired.

However, these measures are more likely to happen in richer, industrialized nations. In poorer countries, there are fewer possibilities of warning, escape and protection. Here, people who lose their jobs, homes, crops and livestock are less likely to recover physically, psychologically and financially.

HERO OR VILLAIN?

Are humans making some natural disasters worse? Are more frequent hurricanes, tornadoes, floods and droughts caused by us burning too many fossil fuels and causing climate change? Are we struggling to tackle the needs of people who have to live with both natural disaster and other disasters, such as poverty and war?

Some developments will hopefully reach most parts of the world. These include new monitoring systems that link networks of Global Positioning Station (GPS) receivers on Earth to GPS satellites in space. Inexpensive sensors are being added to GPS receivers on Earth so that they can pick up both weather and geological measurements. These links between GPS satellites and receivers on Earth will lead to quicker and more accurate warnings. They will enable more effective computer modelling and hazard mapping, too.

> **Meaningful warnings can save lives when issued within one to two minutes of a destructive earthquake, several tens of minutes for tsunamis, possibly an hour or more for flash floods, and several days or more for extreme winter storms.**
>
> Dr Lee C. Gerhard, geologist and defender of fossil fuels

These industrial chimneys are belching out harmful greenhouse gases and pollutants. Is this making our climates less predictable and weather disasters more extreme?

Quiz

How much do you remember about natural disasters from reading this book? You could find out by answering these questions. You can use the index to help you. Some of the answers might lie in the boxes and captions as well as the main text.

1 Many people live in the shadow of a volcano because the soil is very fertile. Which chemical that comes from volcanic matter fertilizes the soil?

   A hydrogen
   B methane
   C nitrogen
   D carbon dioxide

2 Which of these techniques would not help volcanologists measure volcanic activity to predict when they will erupt?

   A using soil testing kits to measure levels of volcanic fertilizer in soils around the volcano
   B using sensors to measure an increase in sulphur dioxide levels in and above the volcano
   C using seismometers to pick up tiny earth tremors
   D using infrared sensors on space satellites to measure heat levels from a volcano

3 Current technology can warn people that an earthquake is about to strike. Up to how much time can they be given to find a place of safety?

   A 60 minutes
   B 24 hours
   C 60 seconds
   D 90 seconds

4 Which is the most damaging stage of an earthquake on land?

   A the second slower tremors
   B the first fast tremors
   C aftershocks in the same place several months later
   D aftershocks in the same place a year later

5 Which of these is the most damaging feature of a hurricane?

   A torrential rainfall
   B tornado
   C hailstorm
   D storm surge

6 What is a hurricane called in the South Pacific Ocean?

A cyclone
B typhoon
C hurricane
D monsoon

7 Which type of equipment can detect tornado formation by measuring patterns of raindrops inside thunderstorm cloud?

A Saffir–Simpson Scale
B Fujita–Pearson Scale
C Doppler Radar
D sonar equipment

8 In the Netherlands, which of these is a new design feature protecting some buildings from flooding?

A tall stilts that allow buildings to stay dry above the floodwaters
B metal shutters fitted to doors and windows
C straps that stop roofs from floating away
D foundations that can float so that the building can be lifted up as floodwaters rise

9 Which of these measures makes drought conditions worse?

A planting trees
B restoring wetlands
C draining wetlands
D seeding clouds with silver iodide chemical

10 How does burning a wide forest roadway, or break, help stop the spread of a forest fire?

A It allows firefighters access to the fire.
B It allows satellite images to monitor the spread of the fire more easily.
C It exposes moisture in the soil, which stops the fire in its tracks.
D It removes vegetation that can catch alight, which stops the fire in its tracks.

ANSWERS: 1C, 2A, 3C, 4A, 5D, 6A, 7C, 8D, 9C, 10D

Glossary

artificial irrigation human-made water sources, such as dams, used for watering plants, especially crops

avalanche very fast flow of snow down a mountain slope

buoy floating device, sometimes with instruments attached. It can float away or be anchored.

computer model computer program that uses data to represent what might happen in a real-life situation, such as future climate conditions

Doppler Radar system that uses pulses of radiation to detect swirling movement in weather patterns and features, such as hurricanes and tornadoes

dormant not active. With a volcano, this means that it could still erupt in the future.

dredge clear out muddy silt that chokes the flow of rivers

geophysicist scientist who studies Earth's movement and magnetism

hazard mapping creating maps that highlight places that are likely to experience a danger, such as a natural disaster. Computer models are often used to create them.

infrastructure service, such as firefighting, or structure, such as a road, that enable an economy or business to operate properly

irrigate supply land with water

lahar volcanic flow of wet debris

marginal at the edge of a place

meteorologist scientist who studies the causes of weather conditions

monsoon shift in wind that brings heavy rain storms to parts of Asia

nitrogen chemical that is found in natural and human-made fertilizers

nuclear fuel radioactive metals, especially uranium and plutonium. They release heat energy when their atoms are split.

pyroclastic flow masses of fast-moving boiling hot liquid rock fragments and gas that flow when part of an erupting volcano collapses

radiation energy released from invisible waves, such as electromagnetic waves. Nuclear radiation is dangerous to the health of living things.

seismologist scientist who studies how the Earth is made up and why it moves. Seismologists collect data on seismic waves that indicate an earthquake.

sonar equipment instruments used to measure depths in water using invisible sound beams or pulses that reflect off surfaces they hit. The time it takes for the beam to return is measured to give depth.

state of emergency when a country or state's government declares an emergency and puts in place plans to help in the disaster or dangerous situation

structural engineer engineer who makes sure that the structure of a building, road or railway is strong enough for its purpose

sulphur dioxide gas that affects the atmosphere and air quality on Earth. Volcanoes give out a lot of sulphur dioxide. So do coal-fired power stations.

telecommunication communicating at a distance using electronic, radio or light signals in systems such as radios, telephones or computers

tsunami huge, high ocean wave pushed up mainly by earthquakes. It can cause disaster when it crashes ashore.

Find out more

If you want to find out more about natural disasters around the world, why not take a look at some of these books and websites.

Books

Fearsome Forces of Nature (Extreme Nature), Anita Ganeri (Raintree, 2013)
Natural Disasters, Claire Watts (Dorling Kindersley, 2012)
Stories About Surviving Natural Disasters (Real Life Heroes), Jen Green (Franklin Watts, 2010)
Tsunamis (Natural Disasters), Richard and Louise Spilsbury (Wayland, 2012)
Wild Weather, (Extreme Nature), Anita Ganeri (Raintree, 2013)

Websites

www.esa.int/esaKIDSen/Naturaldisasters.html
Take a look at this website to find out more about natural disasters, how they affect people and the technology that can help them. There are also news items and fun quizzes.

www.sepakids.com
The Scottish Environment Protection Agency website has a section for children that explains climate change, flooding and waste.

www.watersafetykids.co.uk/pdfs/Flooding.pdf
This website has lots of information about flooding and its effects.

Places to visit

Local and national science and technology museums often hold special exhibitions on the atmosphere, the environment and climate change. You can also check out the following:

Natural History Museum, London
www.nhm.ac.uk/index.html

Witness the drama and trauma of volcanoes and earthquakes unfolding through film, specimens, interactive games and even an earthquake simulator! There is also an Ecology gallery, which shows the impact of humans on our planet and its climate. The Earth Today and Tomorrow gallery looks at wind, wave and solar powered machinery, which could help reduce the wild weather associated with climate change. There is a section on farming methods and how they affect our planet. See the water borehole dug right down into the chalk below the museum!

Science Museum, London
www.sciencemuseum.org.uk

Among the many great science exhibits in this museum there is a display called "Climate Changing Stories". It looks at climate over time through scientific discovery, artefacts and art.

Dynamic Earth, Edinburgh
www.dynamicearth.co.uk/learning

Here, you can find out more about the science of our planet, including climate change, through 3D and 4D technology and interactive exhibitions. Workshops, outdoor activities and a fun zone bring learning to life. You can see how Earth developed over time and how it might evolve in the future. From Space, you can look down at Earth and see in what ways humans have changed the planet.

W5 Science and Discovery Centre, Belfast
www.w5online.co.uk/what-is-w5

Visit the interactive floor shows at this thrilling museum. They include "The Landfill That Time Forgot", which shows what happens when a lorry full of waste is emptied into a landfill site. You will see the effects of the waste and find out how we can stop its harmful emissions, which affect our climate and increase natural weather disasters.

Index